SUPER
STINK-Y STUFF
FROM A to Zzzzz

Megan McDonald   illustrated by Peter H. Reynolds

CANDLEWICK PRESS

A Anatomy of Stink

Anatomy of Stink

HEIGHT:
3 feet 8 inches (shrinks to 3 feet 7 3/4 inches at night)

HAIR:
hair spikes, which help Stink look taller

NOSE:
super sniffer; can smell a corpse flower a mile away

FEET:
live inside some of the world's worst super-stinky sneakers

EYES:
fell asleep on the school bus and made him miss his stop

ARMS:
got stuck in a PJ shirt; punched Webster by mistake

HEAD:
size large, to fit genious brain

BRAIN:
full of encyclopedia facts, especially about things beginning with the letter S

Astro (or Astro-NOT)

ASTROBLEME:
a circle left when a meteorite crashes into Earth

ASTROCOMPASS:
finds true north in relation to the stars and planets

A FEW FACTS ABOUT ASTRO, STINK'S FAVORITE GUINEA PIG:

- has blue eyes
- has spiky hair like Stink
- found hiding out in the Great Wall of China
- took a ride on the Great Guinea Pig Express
- almost became snake food
- hitched a ride in Stink's backpack
- once wore Stink's undies

ASTROCYTE:
a star-shaped cell

FUR-EEKY!

Backpack Backbreakers **B**

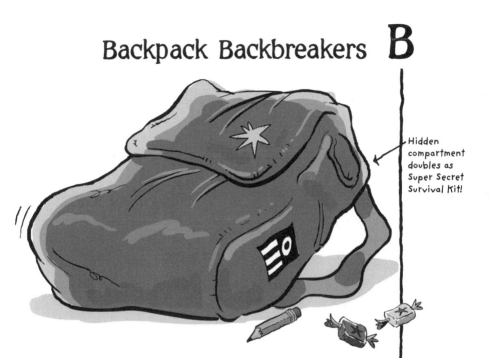

Hidden compartment doubles as Super Secret Survival Kit!

STINK NEVER LEAVES HOME WITHOUT:

- a guide to drawing comics
- a pocket edition of the S encyclopedia
- an old newt skin
- real (not-pirate) money
- a vial of anti-sister repellent
- his Toad Pee Club membership card
- a spare jawbreaker
- his James Madison friendship coin

Backpack Backbreakers

What's in your pack? Take a closer look. . . .

PENS:
A Parker ballpoint pen will produce more than five miles of writing before running out of ink.

PENCIL:
The average pencil can be sharpened seventeen times and write about 45,000 words.

ERASERS:
One hundred years ago, pencils did not have erasers, because teachers thought that they might encourage kids to make mistakes!

GLUE:
The first patented glue was invented in Britain in 1750. It was made from fish!

RULER:
In 1994 scientists in Canada created the world's smallest ruler. The teeny-tiny ruler can measure stuff that is only one-sixtieth of a human hair wide.

CRAYONS:
A kid in the United States will wear down 730 crayons by the time he or she is ten.

DID
YOU
KNOW?

April 15
is Rubber
Eraser Day!

4

Belly Button

While Stink is proud of his belly button, he thinks some things should remain PRIVATE. Judy, on the other hand, has no problem taking Stink's dried-up umbilical cord to school in a jar to show the entire third grade!

Know what omphaloskepsis is?
We've all done it. It's the art of goofing off, staring into space, or contemplating one's navel.

ARE YOU AN INNIE OR AN OUTIE?

Some psychologists believe that your belly button holds a clue about the kind of person you are.

HORIZONTAL:	emotional
VERTICAL:	generous
OUTIE:	optimistic
INNIE:	gentle
OFF-CENTER:	fun-loving
CIRCULAR:	calm, quiet

DID YOU KNOW?

Like your fingerprints, no two belly buttons are alike.

Best Friends

WHAT TO KNOW ABOUT SOPHIE OF THE ELVES (AKA SOPHIE OF THE SMELLS):

- likes hobbits and elves
- won the Golden Clothespin Award for the smelliest sneakers
- once helped Stink make toilet water
- her favorite book starrs a brave mouse and an evil rat
- her favorite saying is "Fur-eeky!"
    - one of her hopes for the future is to have a girl president

Best Friends

WHAT TO KNOW ABOUT WEBSTER
(AKA THE SMELLSTER):

- got sucker-punched during Stink's Attack of the PJs
- had his feelings hurt when Stink forgot about his birthday party
- his favorite book is THE PURPLE SNAIL
- got a Candy-Gram piñata from Stink
- his favorite saying is "Double gross!"

Birthdays and Birth (Oops!) Days

Jeep Baby! Stink made headlines when he was only a minute old, because he was born in the backseat of a Jeep on the way to the hospital.

STINK'S BIRTHDAY:
February 29, Leap Year!

JUDY'S BIRTHDAY:
April 1, April Fools' Day
(This is not an April Fools' joke!)

Other funny places where babies have been born:

- on an elevator
- in a furniture store
- in a taxicab
- in a movie theater
- in a subway station
- at a gas station
- at a barbecue restaurant
- at Disneyland

DID YOU KNOW?

Peter Reynolds's birthday is March 16.

Megan McDonald's birthday is February 28.

8

Brainiac = Brain + Maniac

Stink is a brainy, encyclopedia-reading maniac. His favorite volume? *S* (for "Stink"), of course!

The average adult human brain is 85% water and weighs about 3 pounds. The genius Albert Einstein had a pretty small brain, weighing in at 2.6 pounds.

WANT A BETTER REPORT CARD? EAT MORE BRAIN FOOD!

- Blueberries
- Strawberries
- Spinach
- Tofu
- Tuna fish
- Liver
- Peanut butter & banana sandwich

DID YOU KNOW?

Peppermint has been known to increase brain waves — just by its smell!

C Candyland

One of Stink's favorite hobbies is a trip to the Whistle Stop Candy Shop for Tweezlers, Milk Dudes, Peanut Butter Yucks, Almost Joys and . . . jawbreakers!

CELEBRATE SWEETS ALL YEAR LONG!

January

3rd—National Chocolate-Covered Cherry Day

26th—National Peanut Brittle Day

February

15th—National Gumdrop Day

March

24th—National Chocolate-Covered Raisin Day

April

12th—National Licorice Day

22nd—National Jelly Bean Day

May

15th—National Chocolate Chip Day

PETER REYNOLDS'S FAVORITE CANDY: a tie between Reese's Peanut Butter Cups and Raisinets.

June is National Candy Month!
16th—Fudge Day

July
20th—National Lollipop Day
28th—National Milk Chocolate Day

August
10th—S'mores Day

September
13th—International Chocolate Day
22nd—National White Chocolate Day

October
30th—National Candy Corn Day
31st—National Caramel Apple Day

November
7th—National Bittersweet Chocolate
with Almonds Day

December
7th—National Cotton Candy Day
26th—National Candy Cane Day

MEGAN
McDONALD'S
FAVORITE CANDY:
a tie between
Reese's Peanut
Butter Cups
and Raisinets.
Same-same!

Comics

I'm cuckoo for comics!

KA-POW!

It's true. Stink Moody loves to read comics.

HEY!

He likes to create his own comics even more.

What he likes most of all is imagining himself as **Stink, superhero!**

WOW!

Comics

Comics

Comics

Corpse Flower

The world's biggest and worst-smelling flower is titan arum, aka the corpse flower. Its odor can be so strong that the human nose can detect it more than half a mile away!

16

Duct Tape D

GOT TAPE?

Duct tape, a kid's best friend. Stink loves the stuff and once used it to build the Great Wall of China.

★ Springfield, Missouri, is the duct tape capital of the world. There, more duct tape is sold per person than in any other place in the world.

★ The world's largest roll of duct tape weighs 650 pounds and is 10,384 yards (or 5.9 miles) long! That's the same weight as six baby hippos and longer than 100 football fields!

★ There's a new tape in town—the geckel! Researchers have come up with a tape so sticky, it works underwater. It was inspired by the gecko and the mussel, both of which have amazing "sticky" powers.

DID YOU KNOW?

Duct tape helped save the lives of three astronauts on APOLLO 13.

E E is for _____.

E is Stink's middle initial. Any guesses about what it stands for?

Ebenezer?   Elwin?   Erving?

STINK E. MOODY

Eustace?   Eugene?

Visit www.stinkmoody.com and take a guess!

Encyclopedia

Stink loves to learn facts by reading the encyclopedia. His favorite is the *S* volume. If you want to find out what's in it, turn to page 82!

DID
YOU
KNOW?

Even encyclopedias sometimes make mistakes. Out of all printed English-language encyclopedias, ENCYCLOPAEDIA BRITANNICA has the fewest.

Nobody's Purfickt
See if you can find all of the spelling mistakes purposely printed in this book. Hint: there should only be twenty, counting the one on this page!

(Turn to page 135 for the answers.)

Eu-REEK-a!

Stink is known as The Nose. Whether it squeaks, reeks, or freaks you out, he can smell it a mile away.

STINK'S REEK METER!
1 = not too smelly
10 = bring out the clothespin!

 The tip of the stinkhorn fungus is covered with slime that flies love! To us, it would smell like rotting flesh.
Reek meter rating: 9

 The hairy blossom of the starfish flower from Africa attracts flies and maggots with its nauseating stench. Gag me with a spoon!
Reek meter rating: 7

 What smells like cat diarrhea? *Sauromatum,* a flower that looks like a lizard! Don't give this one for Mother's Day.
Reek meter rating: 8.5

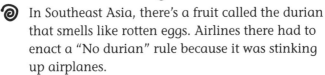 In Southeast Asia, there's a fruit called the durian that smells like rotten eggs. Airlines there had to enact a "No durian" rule because it was stinking up airplanes.
Reek meter rating: 11

F Fur & Fangs

A cat that makes toast? A chicken that plays the piano? One hundred and one escaped guinea pigs? You'll find them all at Stink's local pet shop, Fur & Fangs.

Fur & Fangs

MEET THE MOODY PETS:

MOUSE
- is a cat
- likes mushed-up bananas
- knows how to make toast
- refuses to eat hair-covered prunes

JAWS
- It's a plant . . . it's a pet . . . it's a Venus flytrap! If you feed it dead hamburger, watch out—P.U.!

TOADY
- mascot of the Toad Pee Club
- almost had to wear undies for show-and-tell

NEWTON
- Class 2D's class pet
- state amphibian of "Newt" Hampshire
- took a big journey down the drane

GUESS WHO?

Fur & Fangs

MORE UNUSUAL PETS

• Four-eyed fish can see above and below water at the same time!

• Potbellied pigs were first introduced to the United States from Asia fifteen years ago. They are easy to train, curious, and loving. They're smarter than the smartest dogs and love a good belly scratch.

• If you hear a scream in the night, it's just your pet kinkajou. They're nocturnal, and their shrill call sounds like a bloodcurdling scream.

Fur & Fangs

- The wallaby is a mini kangaroo. They make affectionate, playful, mischievous pets. The wallaby is in the macropod family, which is named for the Latin word meaning "big foot."

- In the 1970s, pet rocks were a real hit. For $3.95, you could buy a rock painted with a tail and a face. The rock came with an owner's manual with hints on how to train your rock to sit, stay, or roll over.

- Stick insects are one of the most popular bugs to keep as pets. They can hide in plain view by looking just like a branch of the plant they'll eat for lunch!

DID YOU KNOW?

In one Native American language, the skunk is called SEGANKU, or "one who squirts."

Stink's grandmother really knows what her grandson likes. When she buys Stink some pajamas, they're not just any pajamas. . . .

"These pajamas are way better than the I ♥ TRUCKS ones I got last year," said Stink. "And the glow-in-the-dark part is kool-with-a-*k*!"

Excerpt from *Stink and the Incredible Super-Galactic Jawbreaker*

Glow in the Dark

Ever wonder how glow-in-the-dark stickers, stars, or even glow-in-the-dark PJs work? They all contain phosphor, a substance that holds light, creating a soft green glow.

★ **JELLYPIGS?**
Scientists at National Taiwan University injected jellyfish protein into pig cells and came up with three green pigs that actually glow in the dark.

★ **WHAT A MOUTHFUL!**
Watch lightning strike—in your own mouth! Go into a dark room, bite down on a hard white wintergreen candy, and watch the sparks fly. Your teeth against the candy make lite through friction. The big, fancy name for this is TRIBOLUMINESCENCE.

★ **HARRY POTTER BY MUSHROOM LIGHT?**
The ghost fungus, a mushroom found in southern Australia, emits a greenish light said to be bright enough to read by!

Guinea Pig Mania

It all began when Stink and his friends discovered three runaway guinea pigs in Webster's backyard. Next thing they knew, they were riding around Virginia with not three but 101 guinea pigs in need of good homes.

Guinea Pig Mania

Do you speak guinea pig? Here's a little guide to help you translate what those little fur balls are saying:

WHEEK! *"I'm so excited!"* or *"I'm lost!"*

BUBBLING *"Pet me,"* or *"Yes, I like that."*

RUMBLING *"I'm the boss!"*

CHUTTING *"Run!"* or *"Help! I'm being chased!"*

CHATTERING *"Warning! Look out!"*

SQUEALING *"Danger, danger!"*

CHIRPING *"I'm so stressed!"*

WEE, WEE, WEE! *"I'm hungry! Feed me!"*

ARR! ARR! *"I'm lonely. Play with me."*

PURRING *"Let's explore; I feel curious."*

PTTP! *"I'm very happy!"*

RRRR! *"Ooh-la-la, I'm in the best mood ever!"*

DID YOU KNOW?

Peter Reynolds had two pet guinea pigs when he was growing up. Their names were Willameena and Christina, and they liked to eat out of the bird feeder with the birds and the squirrels!

Want to hear guinea pig-speak? Try this:

http://www.mgpr.org/MGPR/Guinea%20Pig%20Sounds.htm

Hic!

HIC!

HIC!

HIC!

HIC!

HIC!

HIC!

HIC!

HIC!

A pirate with hiccups? Scurvy Stink gets so excited about finding treasure that he could win the Hiccup Olympics.

Hiccup

Charles Osborne holds the world record for the longest attack of hiccups—sixty-eight years!

Hiccup

It's said that in that time, he hiccupped 430 million times.

Hiccup

Lots of things can cause hiccups. One of the most common causes is eating too fast.

Hiccup

In the olden days, hiccups were thought to be caused by elves.

DID YOU KNOW?

Scientists in France study tadpoles to learn about hiccups in humans.

28

HIC!

CAN YOU GUESS WHICH OF THE FOLLOWING ARE REAL CURES FOR HICCUPS?

☐ Think of all the bald men you can.

☐ Close your eyes and picture a neon sign with the word THINK blinking off and on.

☐ Blow on your thumb.

☐ Scream.

☐ Say "pineapple."

☐ Talk nonstop for ten seconds.

☐ Count to twenty with your fingers in your ears.

☐ Rub your earlobe.

☐ Chew gum.

☐ Balance a spoon on your nose.

☐ Smell a candle.

☐ Eat a Popsicle, dill pickle, or marshmallow.

HIC! *HIC!* *HIC!* *HIC!*

(Turn to page 135 for the answer.)

H Hugh Mongous and Other Huge Stuff

First it was short, shorter, shortest. Then it was gigantic, super-colossal, inter-galactic! Whether its shortest, tallest, stinkiest, or grossest, with Stink, it's always the most-est!

Hugh Mongous

At Ocean View Water Park in Virginia Beach, Stink and his friends get a close-up view of Hugh Mongous, a giant (not real) gorilla dressed like a surfer. *Hang ten, dude!*

Q. *What's bigger than a football field, can be broken into 21,600 pieces, and took 777 people to put together?*

A. The world's largest jigsaw puzzle, built in Hong Kong.

DID YOU KNOW?

In his old age, Benjamin Franklin couldn't reach the books on the top shelf, so he created the "long arm," a contraption with a grasping claw at the end of a long wooden pole.

Hugh Mongous

SEVERAL SUPER SUPERLATIVES

LONGEST WALL: the Great Wall of China, witch has almost four billion bricks and is more than 4,000 miles long.

LARGEST FROG: the African goliath frog, which measures 13.6 inches, nose to tail

LARGEST JELLYFISH: the Arctic lion's mane jellyfish at 7 feet 6 inches; tentacles, 120 feet

HIGHEST JUMP BY A PIG: 27.5 inches

MOST SOCKS WORN ON ONE FOOT: 70

TALLEST SAND CASTLE: 49.55 feet tall

LARGEST UNDIES: 47 feet 3 inches wide

WORLD'S TALLEST (AND FASTEST!) ROLLER COASTER: Kingda Ka near Jackson, New Jersey. Maximum height: 456 feet. Maximum speed: 128 miles per hour.

Hugh Mongous

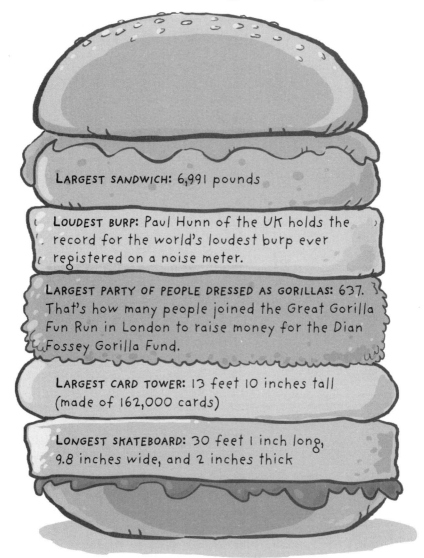

LARGEST SANDWICH: 6,991 pounds

LOUDEST BURP: Paul Hunn of the UK holds the record for the world's loudest burp ever registered on a noise meter.

LARGEST PARTY OF PEOPLE DRESSED AS GORILLAS: 637. That's how many people joined the Great Gorilla Fun Run in London to raise money for the Dian Fossey Gorilla Fund.

LARGEST CARD TOWER: 13 feet 10 inches tall (made of 162,000 cards)

LONGEST SKATEBOARD: 30 feet 1 inch long, 9.8 inches wide, and 2 inches thick

I Idiom

"I am NOT an idiot!" said Judy.
"Id-i-om," said Stink. "It's what you call a funny saying. Like if you're in a bad mood, I could say you got up on the wrong side of the bed."

Excerpt from *Stink and the Incredible Super-Galactic Jawbreaker*

Idiom

Can you match the correct idiom to the illustrations on the next three pages?

1. Feeling like a heel
2. Making a mountain out of a molehill
3. Costing an arm and a leg
4. As cute as a bug's ear
5. Sour grapes

36

C.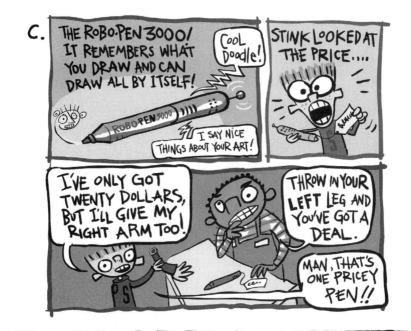

E.

(Turn to page 135 for the answers.) 37

Inventions

A RECIPE FOR ANTI-SISTER REPELLENT BY STINK E. MOODY:

To a jar of toilet water, add a dash of smelly stuff. Voilà! Judy-Moody-Be-Gone! It's almost as good as bug spray.

Inventions (by real kids like you!)

- **LOUIS BRAILLE** was only fifteen when he invented a way for the blind to read and rite by using raised dots.

- **CHESTER GREENWOOD** was seventeen when he invented earmuffs in 1873.

- **GEORGE NISSEN,** at age sixteen, invented the trampoline out of old junk.

- At age eleven, **FRANK EPPERSON** left a stir stick in his soda and it froze. Eureka! The first Epsicle. His kids later changed the name to Popsicle.

- In 1922, **RALPH SAMUELSON** invented waterskiing. He made his first pair of water skis out of slats from barrels at age eighteen.

DID YOU KNOW?

When Peter Reynolds was Stink's age, he invented a time machine. But it was only big enough to fit a mouse. Who knows if the time machine worked? When the mouse got back, all it said was "Squeak"!

J James

"How'd you get the name Stink, anyway?" asked Sophie of the Elves.

"HER," said Stink, pointing to Judy.

"I'll tell it! I'll tell it!" Judy said. "One day, when Stink was a baby, Dad was changing Stink's dirty diaper . . ."

"Eee-yew!" said Webster, pinching his nose.

"Anyway, it was really stinky. So I started singing this song I learned in preschool."

"Don't sing it!" said Stink, covering his ears.

"Sing it!" said Webster and Sophie.

"It sounds like 'Old McDonald Had a Farm.':

> *My little brother smells so bad,*
> *Stinky, stinky poo!*

Ever since then, we called him Stinky Poo," said Judy.

"Then one day, it got shortened to just plain Stink," said Stink.

Excerpt from *Stink and the World's Worst Super-Stinky Sneakers*

Jawbreakers

Stink likes candy. He likes it even better when it's *FREE*.

- A jawbreaker starts with one tiny grain of sugar. The sugar is whirled around and around until it snowballs to the right size.

- It would take an average-size frog approximately two years to digest the world's largest jawbreaker.

OTHER NAMES FOR JAWBREAKERS:

GOBSTOPPER   ANISEED BALL

GRAPESHOT   JAW BUSTERS

FIREBALL   LEMONHEAD

Jawbreakers

Judy

It's not the way Stink would have planned it, but in the Moody family, Judy is the oldest (and tallest) kid, and Stink is the youngest (and shortest).

TEN WAYS TO REALLY BUG YOUR MOODY BIG SISTER:

1. Hide your *smelliest* sneakers under her bed.

2. Repeat everything she says.

3. Have a stare-down contest without telling her.

4. Talk by moving your lips without making any sounds.

5. Take a picture of her while she's sleeping, then show her friends.

6. Steal her mood ring (or dessert!) when she's not looking.

7. Pretend to wipe spit off your face while she's talking.

8. Sing "Happy Birthday to You" when it's not her birthday.

9. Tap a pencil on the table while she's trying to do her homework.

10. Make her pay you a dollar to stop bugging her!

Ka-Ching! K

Stink made fifty cents a bag selling moondust. He tried to charge a quarter just for telling Rocky what Judy said when they had been in a fight. He even got a five-dollar gift certificate just for being short. Stink is always on the lookout for a way to make a buck.

Hand over that clam!

It costs 4.2 cents to make a dollar bill.

NICKNAMES FOR A ONE-DOLLAR BILL:

PAPER

CLAM

BUCK

SMACKEROO

SINGLE

BONE

ONE

GREENBACK

BILL

DEAD PRESIDENT

Karate

Look out. When Stink starts karate-chopping everything from pencils to rulers, it could spell trubble.

★ Karate is thousands of years old. Because weapons were banned in Okinawa for many years, the Japanese learned hand-fighting techniques.

★ The word KARATE comes from two Japanese characters. KARA means "empty" and TE means "hand."

★ The bone in your hand is forty times stronger than concrete. Still, it takes years for karate experts to learn to bust up a piece of wood with their hand.

Letters and Letter Writing L

Greetings, Salutations, P.S.
Stink learns all about writing letters in
Mrs. D.'s class. There's no stopping the
mighty pen of Stink E. Moody.

The oldest message in a bottle spent 92 years and
229 days at sea! The bottle, numbered 423B, was
recovered by fisherman Mark Anderson of the UK
on December 10, 2006.

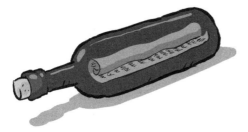

**DID
YOU
KNOW?**

In Canada,
Santa has
his own
postal code:
HOH OHO.

Letters and Letter Writing

"THE MAIL MUST GO THROUGH"

In 1861, the pony express had to speed President Lincoln's inaugural address from St. Joseph, Missouri, to Sacramento, California. Rider "Pony Bob" was shot with an arrow in his arm and one through his jaw, but he kept on riding. He rode 120 miles in eight hours, stopping for only a few minutes to bandage his wounds.

DID YOU KNOW?

The pony express delivered 34,753 letters. Letters were written on lightweight paper and wrapped in oiled silk to protect them from the weather.

Letters and Letter Writing

A DANGEROUS BUSINESS . . .

WANTED

YOUNG, SKINNY, WIRY FELLOWS NOT OVER 18. MUST BE EXPERT RIDERS, WILLING TO RISK DEATH DAILY.

ORPHANS PREFERRED.

PONY EXPRESS

DID YOU KNOW?

Megan McDonald once had a job where she got to transcribe old letters written by George Washington himself. His writing sure was hard to read!

Letters and Letter Writing

Millions of letters from around the world are sent to Santa each year. These countries receive the most:

FRANCE	1.22 million
CANADA	1.06 million
U.S.	1 million
U.K.	750,000
GERMANY	500,000

NORTH POLE, ALASKA, receives more than 120,000 letters to Santa per year.

ROVANIEMI, FINLAND (a town on the Arctic Circle), receives 750,000.

In ROVANIEMI, elves are needed to help Santa answer all the letters. But you have to study at the Elf Academy in order to be one of Santa's helpers. Other duties include wrapping presents, making fires in the snow, and knowing the names of the local wildlife.

Madison, James M

Stink's favorite president, James Madison, is the Shortest President Ever (but still a Big Cheese).

James Madison = 5 feet 4 inches
James "Stink" Moody = 3 feet 8 inches

Do the math! How much shorter is Stink Moody than James Madison?

(Turn to page 136 for the answer.)

James Madison

James Madison was only twenty-five years old when he started to write the Constitution. To make himself look older, he always wore black and put white powder in his hair.

DID YOU KNOW?

James Madison liked ice cream and had a pet parrot.

Moon Rocks

Stink is loony for the moon and finds space far out. He even owns his very own moon rock. Well, he used to own his very own moon rock. . . .

SMASH!

"It's not a moon rock anymore!" cried Stink.

"Look at it this way, Stink," said Judy. "Now you have something better than a moon rock."

"What could be better than a moon rock?" asked Stink.

"Lots and lots of moondust."

Excerpt from *Judy Moody*

DID YOU KNOW?

Moondust is about 50 percent silicon dioxide glass, created when meteorites hit the moon.

52

Moon Rocks

★ The National Cathedral in Washington, D.C., has a special stained-glass window that contains piece no. 230, a tiny bit of rock brought back from the moon by APOLLO 11.

★ 2,415 moon roks were collected by U.S. Apollo missions.

★ A new mineral found on the moon was named armalcolite for three astronauts on APOLLO 11. Can you name the three astronauts?

(Turn to page 136 for the answer.)

DID YOU KNOW?

The oldest rock found so far on Earth is 3.8 billion years old. The oldest moon rock recovered so far is 4.5 billion years old.

Mouse

A cat named Mouse? Only at the Moodys' house! And like the rest of the family, Mouse has her moods.

MOUSE MOOD METER

HAPPY CAT
She's lying on her belly, eyes half-closed, and purring

MAD CAT
She's puffed up and arching her back, flicking her tail from side to side

SCAREDY-CAT
Her ears are flattened, she's crouching, and she avoids eye contact

WORRY CAT
She's flicking her tongue and twitching her ears back and forth

Museums

Stink loves museums almost as much as he loves encyclopedias.

HIS FAVES:

- The Gross-Me-Out exhibit at the science museum

- The Isle of Wight Museum, home of the world's oldest ham

GROSS-ME-OUT
THE WONDERFUL WORLD OF SMELLY STUFF

Museums

CHECK OUT THESE OTHER WAY-COOL, FOR-REAL MUSEUMS:

- THE ALIMENTARIUM FOOD MUSEUM in Switzerland has a 4,200-year-old cake.

- LUNCH BOX MUSEUM, Columbus, Georgia

- BANANA MUSEUM, Hesperia, California
  Home of the petrified banana and a banana phone.

- INTERNATIONAL UFO MUSEUM, Roswell, New Mexico
  Flying saucer? Alien? Weather balloon? Find out about the mysterious crash landing near Roswell, New Mexico, in July 1947.

- COCKROACH HALL OF FAME, Plano, Texas

- MUSEUM OF DIRT, Boston, Massachusetts
  Dirt from Antarctica, not to mention lint donated by author Dave Barry.

- LEILA'S HAIR MUSEUM, Independence, Missouri
  More than 2,000 objects made of human hair.

- MUSÉE DES ÉGOUTS DE PARIS
  Tour the sewers of Paris. P.U.!

DID YOU KNOW?

The Burnt Food Museum in Arlington, Massachusetts, is temporarily closed due to fire damage!

Newts **N**

When Stink brings home his classroom pet, Newton, he learns all there is to know about way-not-boring newts in *Newtsweek* magazine.

DID YOU KNOW?

If a newt loses an eye, it can grow a new one! The same goes for losing a limb, the heart, part of the intestine, or a jaw.

Newts

LIFE CYCLE OF A NEWT:

Newt eggs are
laid in the water.

When fully grown,
a female newt returns
to the water to lay her eggs,
and the cycle starts all over
again.

When the young newts
hatch, they can
breathe only
with gills, so
they spend the
first part of their
lives in the water.

Some newts leave the water for
land at this time and are known
as red efts. They are red-orange at
this stage but turn green as
they mature
over a two to
three-year period.

As the newts grow,
they develop lungs
for breathing air.

Nose

The human nose can detect 10,000 different smells. Stink was born with a very special nose, a super sniffer.

- Most people think birds can't smell. But in fact, they use smells to make a "map" of where to fly.

- An elephant's trunk can smell water from 3 miles away.

- Your nose is at its peak—can smell the most smells—when you are ten years old.

EDWARDO
AND HIS
NOSE MAXIMA

DO YOU HAVE RHINOTILLEXOMANIA?

It's not scurvy.

It doesn't mean you're crazy for rhinos.

It means you're booger-crazy— **can't stop picking your nose.**

DID YOU KNOW?

Your nose produces between one pint and one quart of mucus in one day! That's snot even funny!

O Optical Illusions

Sometimes, Stink feels like a shrimp, a shortcake, a *stunt*-ed man. Stink's sister, Judy, tells him that wearing clothes with up-and-down stripes will give the *illusion* that he is taller than he really is. Check out these other tricks to play on your eyes.

Are these staggered black-and-white stripes exactly the same width from end to end? Get out your ruler and measure!

Optical Illusions

Now try looking at these black-and-white stripes. Are they straight or curved?

Look at these two flowers. Which center spot is bigger, the one in the flower on the left or the one in the flower on the right? Are you sure?

(Turn to page 136 for the answers.)

P Pirates

Scurvy Stink and Mad Molly O'Maggot (Judy Moody) pick up some pirate rules and lingo as they search for treasure on Ocracoke Island, where the real Blackbeard the Pirate once sailed the seas and swung his hammock.

Pirates

SCURVY STINK. MAD MOLLY O'MAGGOT.
Pick a word from each column to
create yer own fearsome name!

Mad	Bones	Archibald
Deadeye	Badfish	Pete
Cutthroat	Ratfink	Pegs
Scurvy	Catfish	John
Bilge	Keelhaul	Obadiah
Black	Coal	Alligator
Sneaky	Gunwales	Baldhead
Jolly	Dirtyfoot	Canker
Slimy	Swordfish	Vulture
Blimey	Buccaneer	Albatross
Iron	Bloody	Ivan
Voodoo	Yardarm	McPhee
Bloody	Crow's Nest	Brigadoon
Grimy	Terrible	Dublin
Dread	Cankersore	Vane
Skylarking	Frosty	Funkhole

Pirates

Tips for talking like a pirate:
Always say "ye" for "you" and "me" for "my." Throw in lots of "Ahoy!" and "Arrr!" The following list will also help you along.

"AHOY!" . . . . "Hello, there!"

"ARRRRRR!" . . . . expression of glee

"AVAST!" . . . . "Hey!" or "Who goes there?"

"BILGE!" . . . . . . "You're nuts!" or "That's crazy!"

"BLIMEY!" . . . . expression of surprise

BOOTY. . . . . loot or money

BUCKO . . . . friend or pal

DAVY JONES'S LOCKER . . . . bottom of the see

DOG . . . . insult, as in "You dog!"

DOUBLOON . . . . a Spanish gold coin

FEED THE FISH . . . . pirate punishment

GRUB . . . . food, eats

Pirates

HEAD . . . . the toilet, the loo

JOLLY ROGER . . . . pirate flag; means "You should surrender!"

LANDLUBBER . . . . non-sailor

ME HEARTIES . . . . pirate captain's crew

MATEY . . . . person or friend

PIECE OF EIGHT . . . . a Spanish silver coin

SCURVY . . . . (1) a disease among sailors caused by lack of vitamin C

. . . . (2) a put-down, as in "Ye scurvy dog!"

SEA DOG . . . . an experienced seaman

"SHIVER ME TIMBERS!" . . . expression of surprise or strong emotion

WALKING THE PLANK . . . . a made-up pirate punishment

"YO-HO-HO!" . . . . Nobody knows what this means, but pirates sure say it a lot.

Pluto

Stink is hopping mad when he learns that Pluto has been demoted from a Planet to a Planet Jr. He's got to learn more about Pluto if he's going to save it.

Pluto, which was considered to be the ninth planet for seventy-five years, flunked a grade in 2006 and is now only a dwarf planet. Its new name is not even a Greek god of the underworld. It's a number: 134340.

Pluto

How do you remember the order of the planets from the sun? This trick used to work wonders.

My Very Educated Mother Just Served Us Nine Pizzas.

Mercury, Venus, Earth, Mars, Jupiter, Saturn, Uranus, Neptune, Pluto.

Now try this:

My Very Educated Mother Just Served Us Nachos.

Mercury, Venus, Earth, Mars, Jupiter, Saturn, Uranus, Neptune, ~~Pluto.~~

Practical Jokes

Fake hand in the toilet. Pickle-flavored gum. Moon rock. Stink and Judy are always playing tricks on each other. Here are a few to try on your friends and family:

◎ Fill a tray of ice cubes with water, dropping a plastic ant, fly, or bug into each section before freezing. Then drop one in someone's lemonade!

◎ Replace the filling in any creme-filled cookie with toothpaste.

◎ Pour hot sauce on your friend's slice of pizza when he or she's not looking.

◎ When your dad goes to sit down, rip a piece of fabric so he'll think he split his plants.

Practical Jokes

 Superglue a quarter to the sidewalk outside your house. Laugh yourself silly when somebody tries to pick it up.

69

Professional Smeller

NOSE JOB!

Stink wants to put his super sniffer to work when he grows up, and become a professional smeller.

What do YOU want to be? Not sure? Turn the page for a few real-life ideas.

DID YOU KNOW?

Professional pig-poop sniffers row, row, row their boats out into the middle of a pond of pig poop to take a whiff and a sample. They test to measure how much methane is produced.

JUDGING
AREA

SPACE

64

Professional Smeller

YOU COULD GROW UP TO BE A:

HAIR-SIMULATION SUPERVISOR
Your job, should you choose to accept it, is to make 3-D hair for animated cartoons! Way cool!

BANANA GASSER
WHA? Yep, you too can spray bananas with a gas that speeds up ripening.

SNAKE MILKER
Animal care experts are hired to extract venom from poisonous snakes by "milking" the reptile's fangs. The venom is then used in serums that treat snakebite.

BANK ROBBER
Hack into computers at banks to help banks learn just how easy or hard it is. That's an order!

BUBBLE POPPER
Get a job testing bubble wrap. It's a blast!

Professional Smeller

MORE REAL-LIFE JOBS TO THINK ABOUT:

HAUNTED-HOUSE ACTOR

JELLY-DOUGHNUT FILLER

UFO TRACKER

MUSHROOM HUNTER

SOCK TURNER

HUMAN CANNONBALL

CHEESE IMPERSONATOR

GLUE CHECKER

PROFESSIONAL SLEEPER

OSTRICH BABYSITTER

GUM BUSTER

(WHO DO YOU THINK REMOVES ALL
THAT ABC GUM FROM UNDER STUFF?)

FORTUNE-COOKIE WRITER

Q Q & A

Test your Stink IQ here:

1. How many freee jawbreakers did Stink get from the jawbreaker company?

2. What award did Stink want to win for the World's Worst Smelly Sneaker Contest?

3. What book was Stink reading for Pajama Day?

4. What is Stink's name in Hawaiian?

5. What is the name of Stink's mailman?

6. What number does Stink wear for Presidents' Day and why?

7. Why is Stink afraid to go to the nurse's office at school?

8. What place does Stink choose to visit on his way to Virginia Beach in the Guinea Pig Express?

SUPER-INTELLIGENT ALL-TIME BONUS QUESTION

Q: What is the name of Stink's six-foot-long stuffed-animal snake?

(Turn to page 136 for the answers.)

Quill Pen

Before there were ballpoint pens, there were quill pens, made from large bird feathers. Goose feathers were the most popular.

Quill Pen

★ The Bible, the Magna Carta, the Declaration of Independence, the Emancipation Proclamation, and the Constitution were all penned using a quill.

★ The Constitution was written with a quill by Jacob Shallus, a Pennsylvania clerk, for a fee of $30 ($325.29 in today's dollars).

★ At the National Archives, pages one and four of the U.S. Constitution are on display in a bullet-proof case. The entire document is displayed once a year on September 17, the anniversary of the day the framers signed the document.

DID YOU KNOW?

The U.S. Supreme Court still uses 1,200 quills a year! This goes back to a tradition that began in 1801.

R Rescue Me!

Q: How many guinea pigs does it take to fill a camper named Squeals on Wheels?

A: *101, rescued by Stink!*

Rescue Me!

OTHER FAMOUS RESCUES

- On April 14, 1912, the ship CARPATHIA rescued 705 TITANIC survivors from their lifeboats in the icy waters of the North Atlantic.

- Faith, a four-year-old rottweiler in Richland, Washington, speed-dialed 911 on the phone when her owner fell and was knocked unconscious.

- In February 1925, a deadly diphtheria epidemic was wiping out the young people of Nome, Alaska. The only medicine that could stop the epidemic was almost 700 miles away. A dog named Balto led a team of sled dogs in a life-or-death race to get the serum through in time to save the children. That famous run led to a yearly dogsled race called the Iditarod.

Rodents

"A funny bone is not a bone.
A prairie dog is not a dog.
And a guinea pig is not a pig—
it's a rodent."

Excerpt from *Stink and the Great Guinea Pig Express*

There are 2,277 species of rodents on all continents but Antarctica.

Forty percent of all mammals are rodents. They have sharp incisors (teeth) and have been around for 65 million years.

DID YOU KNOW?

The smallest rodent in the world today is the African pygmy mouse. The average adult measures just over three quarters of an inch long.

Rodents

- The giant beaver, the giant dormouse, and the Flores giant rat are just a few of the prehistoric rodents that once scurried and scrabbled across the earth.

- A capybara is the largest living rodent. It weighs one hundred pounds, the same wait as President James Madison!

S Secret Codes

Stink and his sister Judy are codebusters. While on an island treasure hunt, they have to crack riddles and secret codes to win pirate booty and a ride on a pirate ship. Take a crack at these super-secret codes:

THE INCHWORM CODE

1. Lay a ruler on a piece of blank paper.

2. Think of your secret message.

3. Beginning with the first letter of your message, write each letter of your message a half inch apart (at the half-inch and inch marks on the ruler.)

4. Lift up the ruler and fill in each gap with random letters to confuse counterspies.

Be sure to let your friend in on the ruler trick so that they can decode your message with a ruler.

Secret Codes

A simpler version of the Inchworm Code is to insert a single random letter between each letter in your message as you write it, like this:

WORD

STINK

JUDY

CODEWORD

SATMIBNRK

JLUWDPYQ

Can you decode the secret message below?

SPKOIMNRKES RMUBLTEX

(Turn to page 136 for the answer.)

Secret Codes

THE BOOKWORM CODE

This secret code uses words borrowed from a book and turns them into numbers. Pretend you want to write a message that has the word GOLD in it. Flip through your chosen book until you find the word GOLD. Write down the following numbers, in this order:

a. Page number

b. Line number

c. Word position in the line

Pretend you found GOLD on page 23, line 4, word 9. The code for the word GOLD would then be **23 4 9.**

Be sure to let your friend know which book he or she needs to have handy in order to decode your message.

Secret Codes

Decode the following secret message using the book STINK AND THE WORLD'S WORST SUPER-STINKY SNEAKERS:

16	1	1
28	12	4
53	5	5
78	5	2
57	5	4
96	8	2

(Turn to page 137 for the answer.)

Short, Shorter, Shortest!

Stink is the shortest person in the Moody family. Imagine his surprise one evening when he discovers that, instead of growing that day, he's shrunk! Chances are that you have too. Want to find out? Here's how:

Have someone measure your height first thing in the morning, then again last thing at night.

ShrinK ShranK ShrunK

By the end of the day, you'll likely be a little shorter than you were first thing in the morning.

Why? During the day, gravity pulls down on your spine, which squeezes out some of the water between the discs in your spine. This water is replaced as you sleep each night. The water works as a cushion between the spinal discs.

DID YOU KNOW?

The shortest man ever was Gul Mohammed of India, who stood only 22.5 inches tall.

Short, Shorter, Shortest!

MORE WAY-COOL SHORT STUFF!

★ In the Galápagos Islands, iguanas actually shrink in length by as much as 20 percent when there's not enough red and green algae to eat. That's like Shaquille O'Neal shrinking from his 7-foot-1-inch height down to 5 foot 8 inches. Even the iguana's bones shrink, not just their cartilage. When the algae return, the iguanas grow again.

★ In the old days, high heels became popular among women and men. This fad started with vertically challenged royalty so they could look taller.

★ During the French Revolution, a man named Richebourg became the shortest spy ever. He stood just 1 foot 11 inches tall and carried secret messages in and out of Paris while disguised as a baby carried by his "nurse."

DID YOU KNOW?

Peter Reynolds was vertically challenged (aka short!) when he was Stink's age. One day he met a girl named Spider who was short too, and they became instant best friends.

88

THE INCREDIBLE SHRINKING BALLOON

You will need:
  1 balloon
  1 glass jar
  1 bowl of ice water

1. Blow up the balloon until it's bigger than the opening in the glass jar.

2. Try to put the balloon into the jar. Won't fit? Place the balloon in the bowl of ice water, and leave it there for a minute or so.

3. Try again. This time the balloon should fit through the mouth of the glass jar.

How did that happen? While hot air expands, cold air contracts or shrinks. When the air inside the balloon was cooled, the balloon shrank, enabling it to fit through the mouth of the jar. Now, that's cool!

Skeletons

Stink does not like visiting the school nurse's office because of Mr. DryBones, the clickety-clackety skeleton hanging in the corner. Creepy!

> "Wait a minute! Stink! I got it! I know what you have!"
> "What?" asked Stink.
> "Skeleton-itis!" said Judy. "Fear-of-Skeletons disease."
>
> Excerpt from *Judy Moody, M.D.: The Doctor Is In!*

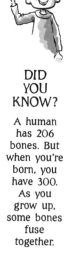

◎ The blue whale skeleton is the largest museum skeleton, found in New Zealand.

◎ The world's largest snake skeleton is that of a 22-foot-long reticulated python at the Cornell University Museum of Vertebrates.

◎ At 42 feet long, Sue, on display at Chicago's Field Museum of Natural History, is the largest T. rex skeleton ever.

DID YOU KNOW?

A human has 206 bones. But when you're born, you have 300. As you grow up, some bones fuse together.

Skinks

Stink loves to read about the skink (rhymes with *Stink!*)—a small cone-headed lizard with shiny scales. Stink gets the skinny on skinks from—what else?—the *S* volume of the encyclopedia.

◎ Skinks can see with their eyes closed! (They have a see-through scale on the lower eyelid.)

◎ The Australian blue-tongued pygmy skink was thought to be extinct until— EUREKA!—in 1992, one was discovered in the belly of a snake.

◎ When a skink is being chased, it can lose its tail to trick the predator. No worries! It can grow a new one.

◎ ACHOO! Skinks sneeze a lot. It's how they clear dirt from their nostrilz.

DID YOU KNOW?

The Solomon Islands giant skink can grow to 28 inches long. That's a lot of skink!

Slime

Gross me out! Stink-o! Skunksville! Where there's smelly stuff, slime cannot be far behind.

- Hippos don't sweat; they slime! Hippo slime keeps hippos from getting sunburned and also kills germs! It starts out clear, turns orange-red, then turns brown!

- Slime eels are covered head to tail in gross, yucky, mucus-y slime! Scientists call them hagfish or slime hags. When a predator gets too close, a slime eel throws out a stream of slime to "Jell-O" the enemy.

Slime

MAKE YOUR OWN
GOOP, GAK, GUNK

You'll need:

1/4 cup cornstarch   4 ounces white glue

1/2 teaspoon borax   1/4 cup warm water

food coloring

1. Sift cornstarch into a big bowl.

2. Add glue and stir (and stir and stir!).

3. In a second bowl, mix the warm water

   with the borax and food coloring.

4. Now add this mixture to the first bowl.

5. Stir well, even after the slime forms.

   You can add several drops of glow-in-the-dark

   paint to make your slime glow.

DID YOU KNOW?

Slugs use their slime to travel upside bown. Slugs have been caught eating their own slime! GROSS!

Snowflakes

Stink wants only one thing for Christmas. One teeny-tiny thing. One puny word. Hardly even a present. And that one thing is . . . SNOW! But it hasn't snowed on Christmas in Virginia for about a hundred years.

Wilson A. "Snowflake" Bentley was the first man to photograph snowflakes and crystals. He made a special microscope-camera that took pictures of these snow formations.

> **Take a look at Snowflake Bentley's snow-crystal museum:**
>
> http://www.bentley.sciencebuff.org/collection.asp

DID YOU KNOW?

Some snow is actually red, green, blue, or black. But snow crystals reflect the full spectrum of light, which makes us see snow as white.

snowflake chart

Sheath

Simple Prism

Solid Column

Cup

Simple Star

Arrowhead Twins

Hexagonal Plate

Hollow Column

Radiating Stinks

12-Branched Star

Crossed Needles

Stellar Plate

Capped Column

Bullet Rosette

Stellar Dendrite

Simple Needle

Sectored Plate

Twin Columns

Isolated Bullet

Radiating Dendrite

Superheroes

Save me,
Mister
Insecto
Magnetic
Doomstopper!

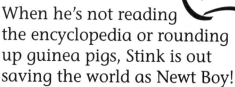

When he's not reading
the encyclopedia or rounding
up guinea pigs, Stink is out
saving the world as Newt Boy!

MAKE UP YOUR OWN SUPERHERO!
(CHOOSE ONE WORD FROM EACH COLUMN.)

Cyber	Mutant	Doomstopper
Super-Atomic	Neutronic	Vulcanoid
Mega-Buster	Android	Buzzernaut
Ultra	Telekinetic	Trashinator
Fatal	Phantom	Scorpio-Blaster
Radioactive	Invisible	Mantis Man
Mr. Insecto	Magnetic	Shrink-O-Tron
The Amazing	Quantum	Invisobot
Shark-O-Matic	Ninja	Zeno-Flash

Superheroes

POSSIBLE SUPERPOWERS:
(CHOOSE THREE.)

X-ray vision

Invisibility

Supersonic hearing

Elasticity

Flying

Underwater breathing

Time warping

Mind control

Energy blasts

Superhuman speed

Ultra-Quantum Trashinator can warp time to throw crime in the garbage!

Not a minute to lose!

The Amazing Phantom Vulcanoid to the rescue!

Superheroes

WHO IS YOUR
SUPERHERO'S
ARCHENEMY
OR NEMESIS?

THE GARBAGE
GREMLIN

SUPER-MOUSE

DOES YOUR SUPERHERO HAVE A
HELPER OR SIDEKICK?

Superheroes

WHAT DOES YOUR SUPERHERO'S COSTUME LOOK LIKE?

POWER PANTS

POWER-T

POWER-SNEAK

↑ POWER-CAPE

JUDY MOODY'S SOCKS

WHAT IS YOUR SUPERHERO'S ONE WEAKNESS?

T Toad Pee Club

When Judy, Rocky, and Frank form a club, Stink is dying to be a member. But he has to pick up a toad. When the toad "pees" on him, he becomes the newest member of the Toad Pee Club. *Eeuw!*

THESE FACTS ARE ALL TOADALLY TRUE!

★ Many toads have poison glands behind their eyes. If a toad is stressed, poison will ooze out of those glands.

★ American toads shed their skin every few weeks. The skin peels off in ONE PIECE. They collect it under their tongue and—GULP!—eat it.

★ IT'S RAINING TOADS!
It actually once rained toads in the town of Villa Angel Flores, Mexico. A small tornado picked up a bunch of toads from a nearby body of water and dropped them all over town. Motorists reported the amphibians falling from the sky at around 11 p.m.

DID YOU KNOW?

Frogs were hopping around during the Jurassic period. (That's about 190 million years ago.) Maybe that's why they have long jumping legs: they saved them from being some dinosaur's lunch!

Toad Pee Club

★ **I'M KNOT KIDDING!**
A group of toads is called a knot. A group of frogs is called an army.

★ **PURPLE TOAD!**
A new toad with neon-bright purple markings, the atelopus toad, was recently discovered in South America.

★ The most common toad you'll find in England is the bufo bufo.

★ The Goliath toad in Cameroon, West Africa, can grow to be as big as a house cat.

★ **NO TOOTHBRUSH NEEDED!**
Frogs have teeth, but toads do not.

TRY THIS TRICKY TONGUE TWISTER:
How many toes does Toady the toad have if a toad has ten toes total?

DID YOU KNOW?
Some frogs can change color according to changes in light, temperature, how wet it is outside, or even . . . mood!

Toad Pee Club

TOAD TICKLERS!

WHERE DO BABY FROGS LEARN TO SWIM?
In a tadpool.

WHAT HAPPENS IF A FROG AND A TOAD BUMP INTO EACH OTHER?
THEY GET TONGUE-TIED.

WHAT DOES A TOAD ORDER IN A RESTAURANT?
French flies and diet croak!

WHY ARE TOADS NORMALLY SO HAPPY?
Because they eat whatever bugs them.

Toilets

A word of advice from Stink:
Always look before you sit!

Wake up. Your toilet's ringing! Not only dead goldfish get flushed. Here's a list of some of the strangest stuff that has been flushed down the toilet:

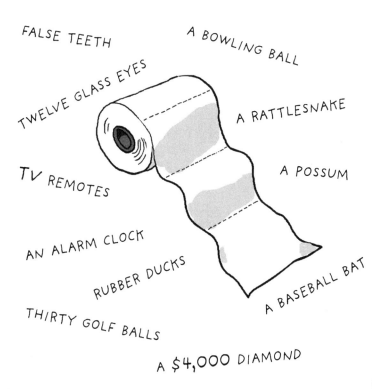

FALSE TEETH

A BOWLING BALL

TWELVE GLASS EYES

A RATTLESNAKE

TV REMOTES

A POSSUM

AN ALARM CLOCK

RUBBER DUCKS

A BASEBALL BAT

THIRTY GOLF BALLS

A $4,000 DIAMOND

DID YOU KNOW?

Every day in Europe, about 270,000 trees are being flushed down the toilet in the form of toilet paper!

Toilets

★ **KEEP THE LID ON!**
More than just fake hands come out of toilets. In one household, an African rock python rose up out of the toilet bowl just as someone was about to sit down! EEK!

★ **THE CORIOLIS FORCE**
Is that a name for the northern lights? The title of a new **STAR WARS** movie? Nope. The Coriolis force explains why water goes down the toilet clockwise in the Northern Hemisphere and counterclockwise in the Southern Hemesphere.

★ **WORLD'S BIGGEST MUSICAL TOILET?**
Chongqing, China, has opened a free, four-story public restroom with 1,000 toilets, possibly the world's largest. Here, you can listen to soothing music or watch TV while you go about your business.

Toilets

FAMOUS FIRSTS
The first flush toilet is 3,700 years
old. No lie. It was built in Greece,
on the Isle of Crete, for the queen.

★ **HEY, WHIZ KID!**
Amsterdam is the proud home of a
talking toilet. Creator Leonard van
Munster has connected a public toilet
to a computer. The toilet can ask you
to lift the seat, warn you about germs,
or make fun of you if you don't wash
your hands. It's
a nonsmoking
toilet, too. Light
up and the toilet
will actually start
coughing and
warn you
about the
hazards
of smoking.

105

U Unbelievable . . . or Not

Stink is the King of Fake Outs. Believe it . . . or not? Take this True *(Way)* or False *(No Way)* Quiz to find out how easy it is to fool you.

1. Masai warriors in Kenya spit at each other to say hello.

2. An asteroid bigger than an aircraft carrier ship hit Earth at the speed of 46,000 miles per hour on March 23, 1989.

Unbelievable . . . or Not

3. A mouse has more bones in its body than a human.

NO WAY!   WAY!

4. Donald Duck's middle name is Fattybottom.

NO WAY!   WAY!

5. Sir Thomas Overbury ate diamonds when he was locked up in the Tower of London for one hundred days.

NO WAY!   WAY!

Unbelievable . . . or Not

6. The tornado sound in the movie **TWISTER** was made by a moaning camel.

   NO WAY!   WAY!

7. A mosquito has forty-seven teeth.

   NO WAY!   WAY!

8. A man survived a great white shark attack by jamming his surfboard down the shark's throat.

   NO WAY!   WAY!

Unbelievable . . . or Not

9. In Pennsylvania, 30,000 people have signed a petition to change Groundhog Day to Whistlepig Day.

NO WAY!   WAY!

10. Vexillology is the study of vampires.

NO WAY!   WAY!

11. An office chair with wheels will travel 5 miles a year.

NO WAY!   WAY!

(Turn to page 137 for the answers.)

Underwear

Okay, let's face it. Underwear is just plain . . . funny. Especially when your guinea pig gets into your clothes and ends up being chased around the room with tighty whities on his head!

★ **SKIVVIES FOR THE AFTERLIFE**
Loincloths were the first underwear. King Tut was buried with 145 of them.

★ **RING IN THE NEW YEAR!**
In Italy, wear red undies to ring in the new year. In Argentina, wear pink.

★ **UNDERWEAR ELF**
In 2005, a teenager heard that one of the things poor people need most is underwear. She inspired people to donate 2,200 brand-new pairs of socks and undies to the Salvation Army.

★ **READ ALL ABOUT IT**
In the Middle Ages, more people began wearing undies. As the undies wore out, the cloth was recycled to make paper. And the paper was used to make books.

DID YOU KNOW?

Since 2003, people in New York City have been celebrating National Underwear Day in early August.

V Ventriloquism

Ever since Stink saw a talking toilet brush on TV, he's wanted to make things talk without moving his lips.

◎ Ventriloquists make a dummy or puppet appear to talk by not moving their own lips as they speak.

◎ B, M, and P are the hardest letters to make without your lips touching. Try it in a mirror. How do ventriloquists get around this? They replace B's with G's, turning "bottle" into "gottle."

Ventriloquism

FAMOUS VENTRILOQUISTS AND THEIR DUMMIES

Edgar Bergen had Charlie McCarthy.
Shari Lewis had Lamb Chop.
Buffalo Bob Smith had Howdy Doody.
Fred Russell had Coster Joe.

OTHER DUMMIES:
- Knucklehead Smiff
- Rodney Duckerfield
- José Jalapeño
- Mortimer Snerd

Virginia

My name is Stink and I come from . . .
Cuckoo?

Stink and Judy Moody live in the state
of Virginia. But the author, Megan
McDonald, has to think up a fake
name for their town. Here are some REAL
names of REAL towns in Virginia. No lie!

Antlers	Hurricane
Bagdad	Joe Neets
Ben Hur	Kermit
Bosses	Lick Skillet
Bumpass	Lipps
Butts	Moon
California	Moonlight
Clam	Mutt
Croaker	Needmore
Cuckoo	Nuttsville
Delaware	Ordinary
Eureka	Peach Bottom
Fries	Pocket
Frogtown	Short Pump
Goochland	Simplicity

Virginia

MOODYVILLE?

What would you call Stink's hometown?
Here are some other real names of towns
to get you started:

Burnt Corn, ALABAMA
Chicken, ALASKA
Unalaska, ALASKA
Flippin, ARKANSAS
Wimp, CALIFORNIA
Chicken Head, FLORIDA
Two Egg, FLORIDA
Monkey's Eyebrow, KENTUCKY
Bald Head, MAINE
Boring, MARYLAND
Embarrass, MINNESOTA
Frankenstein, MISSOURI
Worms, NEBRASKA
Zap, NORTH DAKOTA
Worstville, OHIO
Ding Dong, TEXAS

W Whisperers

Guinea pig whisperer: (n.) a person, like Stink, who has a natural ability to understand and communicate with guinea pigs

There are many kinds of "whisperers" in the world.

★ Heather Mayers is an iguana whisperer. At the zoo in Syracuse, New York, she coaxed Cy, a dying 5-foot-long iguana, back to health.

★ The first horse whisperer was Daniel Sullivan, an Irishman in the 1800s who could "gentle" the most out-of-control horses in a secret way, as if he spoke their language.

★ Ian Gordon is called a shark whisperer. He's been swimming with great whites for almost thirty years.

★ Cindy Wegner of Hershey, Pennsylvania, gets paid to talk to praying mantises. She's an animal communicator, someone who claims to know what animals are thinking and feeling.

Whisperers

HERE ARE A FEW HELPFUL FACTS FOR THE WOULD-BE WHISPERER:

- Chimps say hello by touching hands.
- Elephants show affection by entwining trunks.
- Gorillas stick out their tongues when angry.
- Horses rub noses.

Who's Who?

Mom
Stink's mom.
Knows a thing or two
about toilet water.

Judy
Big sister.
The mudiest of all.

Webster
(NOT the dictionary.)
Best friend.

Sophie
(Real name, Elizabeth.)
Other best friend.

Who's Who?

Stink
Star of the show.
Super sniffer.

Mrs. Dempster
Stink's second grade teacher.
Queen of Pajama Day.

?
coming soon . . .

Dad
Stink's dad.
The Piñata Papa.

Mrs. Birdwistle
Owner of Fur & Fangs.
Guinea pig heroine.

X X Marks the Spot

What does *x* have to do with Stink?
Not much. But what's an encyclopedia
without it? Guess which *x* words are real
words. Hey! No peeking at the dictionary!

xantaphon: (n.) a rare hummingbird from
  Xanto, China

xebec: (n.) a small ship with three masts

xenatrog: (n.) a rare desert amphibian

xenolith: (n.) a piece of rock included in
  another rock

Xenon: (n.) a planet formed by kryptonite in
  Superman comics

xenotech: (n.) a computer expert in xeno-
  transporting

X Marks the Spot

xeroderma: (n.) a disease that turns the skin flaky like fish scales

xeromorphic: (n.) a name for plants specially adapted to survive in the desert

xerocitis: (n.) an inability to remember the number zero brought on by brain-freeze

xycron: (n.) a unit of measure that equals 100 cronos

xylomatic: (n.) a robotic xylophone that plays up to three hundred tunes automatically

X-ray star: (n.) a star in the heavens that emits radioactive rays

(Turn to page 137 for the answers.)

Y Yeti (Y not? What else is there?)

The yeti is a giant hairy creature rumored to live in the Himalayas. It's also known as the abominable snowman, Sasquatch, or bigfoot.

★ In 1961, Nepal declared that the yeti did exist and adopted it as their national symbol. They even honored the yeti on a postage stamp.

★ A yeti cousin might be a yowie. A yowie is a hairy, gorilla-like cross between a lizard and an ant. Also called a bunyip.

Yeti

REMARKABLE YETI QUALITIES:

★ whistles and growls, or roars like a lion

★ tosses huge stones as if they were pebbles

★ can kill with a single punch

★ stands between 7 and 10 feet tall

★ has reddish hair and a terrible smell

Z Zero

$$5 \times 0 = 0$$

Stink is really good at math. Actually, he's really good at just about everything having to do with school. In honor of Stink's big brain, meet the number zero!

$$9 \times 0 = 0$$

Million has 6 zeros
Billion has 9 zeros
Trillion has 12 zeros
Quadrillion has 15 zeros
Septillion has 24 zeros
Nonillion has 30 zeros
Decillion has 33 zeros
Undecillion has 36 zeros
Duodecillion has 39 zeros
Quattuordecillion has 45 zeros
Octodecillion has 57 zeros
Novemdecillion has 60 zeros
Centillion has 303 zeros

$$0 \times 0 = 0$$

$$11 \times 0 = 0$$

$4 \times 0 = 0$

The word **googol,** a number with 100 zeros, was thought up in 1920 by a nine-year-old.

100,000,000,000,000,000,000,000,
000,000,000,000,000,000,000,000,
000,000,000,000,000,000,000,000,
000,000,000,000,000,000,000,000,
000,00

$7 \times 0 = 0$

Oops!
The Web search engine Google was named after this number, but it was accidentally misspelled.

A googolplex is not a movie theater with a hundred screens. It's the number 1 follwed by a googol of zeros.

$8 \times 0 = 0$

Zzzzz's

COUNTING ZZZ'S

Stink was catching zzz's on the bus one day when he missed his stop.

Check out these other sleep-related facts.

AMAZZZING!

⊚ People have been known to take catnaps with their eyes open. (Maybe they should be called fishnaps, since fish always sleep with their eyes open.)

⊚ Ducks afraid of being preyed upon sleep by keeping one-half of their brain awake while the other half sleeps. Dolphins are half-brainers, too!

DID YOU KNOW?

The record for staying awake is 18 days, 21 hours, and 40 minutes, during a rocking-chair marathon.

Zzzzz's

◎ Teenagers need as much sleep as babies and small children.

◎ Counting sheep actually does help people fall asleep. Counting toads or guinea pigs works just fine, too. But guess what? Imagining a waterfall or beach will make you fall asleep even faster!

◎ It's the law! In Oklahoma, it's against the law to sleep on a refrigerator that's outdoors.

◎ In Alaska, it's against the law to wake up a sleeping bear to take its picture.

THE SLEEPYHEAD AWARD GOES TO . . .

BATS! Brown bats sleep 20 hours a day.

Here's how other animals rate:

Python	18 hours
Tiger	16 hours
Hamster	14 hours
Cat	12 hours
Pig	8 hours
Cow	4 hours
Horse	3 hours
African elephant	3 hours

The ostrich sleeps only 15 minutes at a time!

Wondering which books inspired the entries in *Stink-O-Pedia*? Take a look! How many of them have *you* read?

Stink: The Incredible Shrinking Kid

Anatomy of Stink
Backpack Backbreakers
Best Friends
Comics
Fur & Fangs
Madison, James
Newts
Optical Illusions
Q & A
Short, Shorter, Shortest!
Slime
Superheroes

Stink and the Incredible Super-Galactic Jawbreaker

Backpack Backbreakers
Candyland
Glow in the Dark
Idiom
Jawbreakers
Letters and Letter Writing
Q & A

Stink and the World's Worst Super-Stinky Sneakers

Anatomy of Stink
Backpack Backbreakers
Best Friends
Corpse Flower

Eu-REEK-a!
Inventions
James
Museums
Nose
Professional Smeller
Q & A
Slime

Stink and the Great Guinea Pig Express

Astro (or Astro-NOT)
Duct Tape
Fur & Fangs
Guinea Pig Mania
Hugh Mongous and Other Huge Stuff
Museums
Rescue Me!
Rodents
Underwear
Whisperers

Judy Moody

Fur & Fangs
Ka-Ching!
Moon Rocks
Practical Jokes
Toad Pee Club
Toilets
Virginia

And look for these other Stink-y topics in forthcoming books about Stink E. Moody:

Karate
Pluto
Ventriloquism
Yeti

Selected Sources

Books:

The Bathroom Readers' Institute. *Uncle John's Strange and Scary Bathroom Reader for Kids Only!* Ashland, OR: Bathroom Readers' Press, 2006.

Branzei, Sylvia. *Grossology*. Illustrated by Jack Keely. New York: Price Stern Sloan, 2002.

Buckley, James, and Robert Stremme. *Scholastic Book of Lists, New and Updated*. New York: Scholastic Reference, 2006.

Glenday, Craig, ed. *Guinness World Records 2007*. New York: Bantam Books, 2007.

Janeczko, Paul B. *Top Secret: A Handbook of Codes, Ciphers, and Secret Writing*. Illustrated by Jenna LaReau. Cambridge, MA: Candlewick Press, 2004.

Johnson, Anne Akers. *The Buck Book*. Palo Alto, CA: Klutz, 1993.

Jones, Charlotte Foltz. *Accidents May Happen*. Illustrated by John O'Brien. New York: Delacorte Press, 1996.

———. *Mistakes That Worked*. Illustrated by John O'Brien. New York: Doubleday, 1991.

Joyce, C. Alan, ed. *The World Almanac for Kids 2008*. Mahwah, NJ: World Almanac Books, 2008.

Masoff, Joy. *Oh, Yikes! History's Grossest, Wackiest Moments*. Illustrated by Terry Sirrell. New York: Workman Publishing, 2006.

———. *Oh Yuck! The Encyclopedia of Everything Nasty*. Illustrated by Terry Sirrell. New York: Workman Publishing, 2000.

Mooney, Julie, and the editors of Ripley's Believe It or Not! *The World of Ripley's Believe It or Not!* New York: Black Dog and Leventhal, 1999.

Morgan, Matthew, and Samantha Barnes. *Children's Miscellany Too: More Useless Information That's Essential to Know*. Illustrated by Niki Catlow. San Francisco: Chronicle Books, 2006.

Rowen, Beth. *Time for Kids Almanac 2008*. New York: Time for Kids Books, 2008.

Selected Sources

Stillman, Janice, ed. *The Old Farmer's Almanac for Kids*. Dublin, NH: Yankee Publishing, 2005.

Swain, Ruth Freeman. *How Sweet It Is (and Was): The History of Candy*. Illustrated by John O'Brien. New York: Holiday House, 2003.

Szpirglas, Jeff. *They Did What?! Your Guide to Weird and Wacky Things People Do*. Illustrated by Dave Whamond. Toronto: Maple Tree Press, 2005.

Taplin, Sam, and Stephen Wright. *The Usborne Official Pirate's Handbook*. Illustrated by Ian McNee. Tulsa, OK: Usborne Books, 2007.

Terban, Marvin. *Scholastic Dictionary of Idioms*. New York: Scholastic, 1996.

Tucker, Tom. *Brainstorm! The Stories of Twenty American Kid Inventors*. Illustrated by Richard Loehle. New York: Farrar, Straus and Giroux, 1995.

Wulffson, Don L. *The Kid Who Invented the Popsicle: And Other Surprising Stories About Inventions*. New York: Cobblehill Books, 1997.

Websites:

Bentley Snow Crystal Collection of the Buffalo Museum of Science. "Primary Collection." http://www.bentley.sciencebuff.org/collection.asp (accessed June 11, 2008).

The Duct Tape Guys. "The Ultimate Books on Tape." http://www.ducttapeguys.com (accessed June 11, 2008).

Graham's Paddock. "The Incredible World of Navel Fluff Part 1: The Collection." http://www.feargod.net/fluff.html (accessed June 11, 2008).

National Confectioners Association. http://www.ecandy.com (accessed June 11, 2008).

Smithfield and Isle of Wight Convention and Visitors Bureau. "Attractions." http://www.smithfield-virginia.com/attractions.html (accessed June 11, 2008).

Space Mart. "World's Forests Being Flushed Down the Toilet." http://www.spacemart.com/reports/Worlds_Forests_Being_Flushed_Down _The_Toilet.html (accessed June 11, 2008).

Answers

p. 18: Encyclopedia

The twenty spelling mistakes in this book can be found on these pages:

1	*genious* should be *genius*
6	*starrs* should be *stars*
18	*Purfickt* should be *Perfect*
21	*drane* should be *drain*
25	*lite* should be *light*
32	*witch* should be *which*
39	*rite* should be *write*
45	*YU* should be *YOU*
46	*trubble* should be *trouble*
53	*roks* should be *rocks*
64	*see* should be *sea*
68	*plants* should be *pants*
74	*freee* should be *free*
81	*wait* should be *weight*
88	*faller* should be *taller*
91	*nostrilz* should be *nostrils*
93	*bown* should be *down*
104	*Hemesphere* should be *Hemisphere*
112	*hips* should be *lips*
118	*mudiest* should be *moodiest*

p. 29: Hic!

All of the above!

pp. 35–37: Idiom

1. D   Feeling like a heel
2. A   Making a mountain out of a molehill
3. C   Costing an arm and a leg
4. E   As cute as a bug's ear
5. B   Sour grapes

Answers

p. 51: Madison, James

If Stink is 3 feet 8 inches tall (44 inches) and James Madison is 5 feet 4 inches tall (64 inches), then Stink is 1 foot 8 inches, or 20 inches (64 inches – 44 inches = 20) shorter than James Madison.

p. 53: Moon Rocks

The mineral armalcolite was named for Neil **Arm**strong, Buzz **Al**drin, and Michael **Coll**ins.

pp. 60–61: Optical Illusions

The staggered black-and-white stripes are exactly the same width from end to end.

The vertical black-and-white stripes are perfectly parrallel, perfectly straight

The dot in the center of the flower on the right is bigger than the dot in the center of the flower on the left.

pp. 74–75: Test Your Stink IQ

1. 21,280
2. The Golden Clothespin Award
3. *Skeletons in My Closet!*
4. Kimo
5. Jack Frost
6. Number 4, because James Madison was the fourth president
7. He has Skeleton-itis, Fear-of-Skeletons disease
8. Smithfield, home of the World's Biggest Ham
★ Super-Intelligent All-Time Bonus Question: Fang

p. 83: Secret Codes

Skinks Rule

Answers

p. 85: Secret Codes
You smell like a corpse flower

pp. 106–109: Unbelievable . . . or Not
1. **Way!** Masai warriors often spit as a greeting!
2. **No way!** The asteroid missed Earth by about six hours.
3. **Way!** A human adult has 206 bones in its body. A mouse has more than 350—as many as an elephant!
4. **No way!** His middle name is Fauntleroy.
5. **Way!** He was poisoned with nitric acid, hemlock, and ground-up diamonds.
6. **Way!** The sound of the camel's moan was slowed down and used as the sound of the tornado.
7. **Way!** The teeth are used to cut into the skin and produce an increased blood flow.
8. **Way!** It happened in 1991.
9. **No way!** But *whistlepig* is another name for groundhog.
10. **No way!** Vexillology is the study of flags.
11. **No way!** It actually travels MORE—about 7 to 8 miles per year!

pp. 120–121: X Marks the Spot
The real words are: xebec, xenolith, Xenon, xeroderma, xeromorphic, X-ray star

First edition 2009

Library of Congress Cataloging-in-Publication Data is available.
Library of Congress Catalog Card Number 2008935651
ISBN 978-0-7636-3963-1

2 4 6 8 10 9 7 5 3

Printed in the United States of America

This book was typeset in Stone Informal, Providence Sans, Beta Bold, and Ashyhouse.
The illustrations were created digitally.

Candlewick Press
99 Dover Street
Somerville, Massachusetts 02144

visit us at www.candlewick.com

CHECK IT OUT!

I have my own place
in cyberspace.

Come visit!

www.stinkmoody.com